THE AFRICAN AMERICAN
EXPERIENCE
FROM SLAVERY TO THE PRESIDENCY

SLAVERY
IN
AMERICA

EDITED BY
CIARA CAMPBELL

Britannica®
Educational Publishing

IN ASSOCIATION WITH

ROSEN
EDUCATIONAL SERVICES

Published in 2016 by Britannica Educational Publishing (a trademark of Encyclopædia Britannica, Inc.) in association with The Rosen Publishing Group, Inc.
29 East 21st Street, New York, NY 10010

Distributed exclusively by Rosen Publishing.
To see additional Britannica Educational Publishing titles, go to rosenpublishing.com.

First Edition

Britannica Educational Publishing
J. E. Luebering: Director, Core Reference Group
Anthony L. Green: Editor, Compton's by Britannica

Rosen Publishing
Hope Louri Killcoyne: Executive Editor
Ciara Campbell: Editor
Nelson Sá: Art Director
Nicole Russo: Designer
Cindy Reiman: Photography Manager
Karen Huang: Photo Researcher

Library of Congress Cataloging-in-Publication Data

Slavery in America/edited by Ciara Campbell.—First edition.
        pages cm.—(The African American experience: from slavery to the presidency)
Includes bibliographical references and index.
ISBN 978-1-68048-036-8 (library bound)
1. Slavery—United States—History—Juvenile literature. 2. Slave insurrections—United States.
3. Antislavery movements—United States—History—19th century—Juvenile literature. 4. African Americans—History—To 1863—Juvenile literature. I. Campbell, Ciara.
E441.S6323 2015
306.3'620973—dc23

2014039198

Manufactured in the United States of America

Photo credits: Cover (Frederick Douglass) Everett Historical/Shutterstock.com; cover (background), pp. 50–51, 61 Hulton Archive/Getty Images; pp. 5 DEA/M.Seemuller/De Agostini/Getty Images; pp. 9, 10–11 De Agostini/Getty Images; pp. 13 Private Collection/ © Michael Graham-Stewart/Bridgeman Images; pp. 14–15 Time Life Pictures/Mansell/The Life Picture Collection/Getty Images; pp. 18–19 Private Collection/The Stapleton Collection/Bridgeman Images; p. 21 Three Lions/Hulton Archive/Getty Images; pp. 22–23 Private Collection/ © Look and Learn/Bridgeman Images; pp. 24–25 Library of Congress Prints and Photographs Division; pp. 26–27, 32, 44–45, 57, 63 MPI/Archive Photos/Getty Images; p. 33 Jupiterimages/Stockbyte/Getty Images; p. 34 Library of Congress Rare Book and Special Collections Division; pp. 36–37 Private Collection/Peter Newark American Pictures/Bridgeman Images; p. 39 © Andy Murphy/Alamy; p. 40 Stock Montage/Archive Photos/Getty Images; p. 42 Fotosearch/Archive Photos/Getty Images; p. 48 J.R. Eyerman/The Life Picture Collection/Getty Images; pp. 52–53 Newberry Library, Chicago, Illinois, USA/Bridgeman Images; p. 54 Universal Images Group/Getty Images; interior pages background texture © iStockphoto.com/ Piotr Krześlak.

CONTENTS

INTRODUCTION

Olaudah Equiano, a self-proclaimed West African who was sold into slavery and later freed, wrote the first slave narrative to become an international best seller. In his two-volume autobiography, *The Interesting Narrative of the Life of Olaudah Equiano; or, Gustavus Vassa, the African, Written by Himself* (1789), he traces his life from boyhood in West Africa, through the dreadful transatlantic Middle Passage and years of slavery in the New World, to eventual freedom and economic success as a British citizen:

> The first object which saluted my eyes when I arrived on the coast was the sea, and a slave ship, which was then riding at anchor, and waiting for its cargo. These filled me with astonishment, which was soon converted into terror when I was carried on board. I was immediately handled and tossed up to see if I were sound by some of the crew; and I was now persuaded that I had gotten into a world of bad spirits, and that they were going to kill me....When I looked around the ship

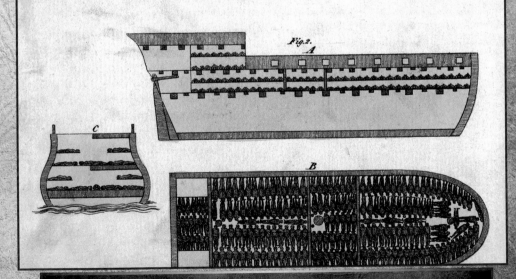

Top: African slave traders kidnap fellow Africans from a village. Bottom: An 18th-century print illustrates how Africans were inhumanely crammed into slave ships during the slave trade.

too and saw a large furnace or copper boiling, and a multi-
tude of black people of every description chained together,
every one of their countenances expressing dejection and
sorrow, I no longer doubted of my fate; and, quite over-
powered with horror and anguish, I fell motionless on the
deck and fainted. When I recovered a little I found some
black people about me....I asked them if we were not to
be eaten by those white men with horrible looks, red faces,
and loose hair.

Documents discovered at the turn of the 21st century, which suggest that Olaudah Equiano may have
been born in North America, have raised ques-
tions, still unresolved, about whether his accounts
of Africa and the Middle Passage are based on mem-
ory, reading, or a combination of the two.

    Nevertheless, this account of the life of a former
slave and others like it comprise one of the most
influential traditions in American literature. With the
rise of the abolition movement in the early 19th century came a demand for hard-hitting eyewitness
accounts of the harsh realities of slavery in the
United States. Narratives by Frederick Douglass
(1845), William Wells Brown (1847), Sojourner Truth
(1850), Solomon Northup (1853), and Harriet A.
Jacobs (1861), among numerous others, claimed
thousands of readers in England and the United
States. These works were written mostly to docu-
ment slavery and to help in the abolitionists' cause
of ending the cruel, inhumane, and degrading institution of human bondage.

    In this illuminating book, the origins of the slave
trade in Africa and the effects of the practice of

slavery on the political and economic history of the United States are explored. King Cotton, the slave hierarchy on southern plantations and the relationship of the slaveholders and slaves, the slave codes that regulated the absolute control of slaves, the ensuing slave rebellions, and the abolitionist movement and those who spoke out against the atrocities of slavery are among the many topics examined in *Slavery in America*.

CHAPTER ONE

SLAVERY AND THE ATLANTIC SLAVE TRADE

The most common form of forced labor in the history of civilization is slavery. "Servitude" is the general term used to describe all types of forced labor. It is derived from the Latin noun *servus*, which really means "slave," though it is recognizable as the source of "servant," too.

In slavery, the laborer is considered property. He or she can be bought and sold like any other commodity. The origins of slavery are unknown, but it probably emerged as an economic necessity or convenience when people began to establish permanent communities based on agriculture.

In the 2nd century CE the Roman lawyer Florentinus said: "Slavery is an institution of the law of nations, whereby a man is—contrary to nature—subjected to the ownership of another." Slavery was thus accepted as legal despite its being considered contrary to natural law. This suggests that after slavery had been in existence for some time, people found convenient rationalizations for it. These were written into law and became established features of nearly every early civilization.

THE ORIGINS OF SLAVERY IN AFRICA

Slavery was practiced in Africa long before the arrival of Europeans on the continent.

The ancient Egyptians enslaved people, and slavery was an important form of labor in the Roman Empire and in the Muslim states. Slaves have also been

This sculptural relief of Nubian slaves is located in the Tomb of Horemheb in Memphis, Egypt, from the 18th Dynasty (New Kingdom).

owned in black Africa through-out recorded history. Black slaves exported from sub-Saharan Africa were widely traded through-out North Africa and the Middle East beginning with the arrival of Muslim traders in these regions. Slave traders most likely marauded nearby villages to obtain slaves. Black Africans were traded across the Sahara, across the Red Sea (from Ethiopia and Somalia), and out of East Africa to supply the Islamic world and the Indian Ocean region with slaves.

Thus, the Europeans who came to Africa continued a well-established tradition of sell-ing human beings as slaves to work for others. Europeans first appeared along the African coast during the late 15th century, when improvements in the technol-ogy of ocean travel made long voyages possible.

In Europe, slavery had nearly died out in the Middle Ages. It was revived by Portugal in the mid-15th century. The Portuguese populated their colonies in the islands off the coast of western Africa largely with black slaves and took many back to Portugal. When Spain and Portugal began establishing colonies in the New World around 1500, they initially forced the local Indians to work their plantations. The

Slaves extract sugar from sugar cane at this mill in the Antilles Islands in the West Indies. British and French possessions in the West Indies used slave labor imported from West Africa for their sugar and coffee plantations.

violence of conquest, however, combined with the impact of European diseases, devastated Indian populations.

The result was a labor shortage that caused the Europeans to look to Africa for a solution. In the Spanish West Indies and in Portuguese Brazil, Indian slaves were gradually replaced by Africans. The Portuguese dominated European activity on the African coasts during the 16th century. In West Africa, the Dutch, French, and British established outposts and forts to compete with the Portuguese.

It was not until the development of sugar, cotton, and tobacco plantations in the Americas that the Atlantic slave trade reached huge proportions,

THE DEMAND FOR MALE SLAVES

The Atlantic slave trade changed the nature of African slavery. Within Africa, slaveholders wanted primarily women and children for labor and for incorporation into their societies. They tended to kill males because they were troublesome and likely to flee. The Europeans, however, demanded primarily adult males to work in the New World colonies. Thus, African rulers began selling males into the international slave trade. Most slaves were captured in raids on neighboring African peoples, though others became slaves because of criminal convictions or failure to pay debts (often not their own). African rulers transported the captives to the coast and kept them in holding pens until they could be sold to European ship captains who sailed up and down the coast looking for slave cargo.

exceeding any such earlier trade. The British became the major traders in slaves, although the French, the Dutch, and others also took part.

THE ATLANTIC SLAVE TRADE

The Atlantic slave trade has been called the triangular trade because it had three stages that roughly form the shape of a triangle when viewed on a map.

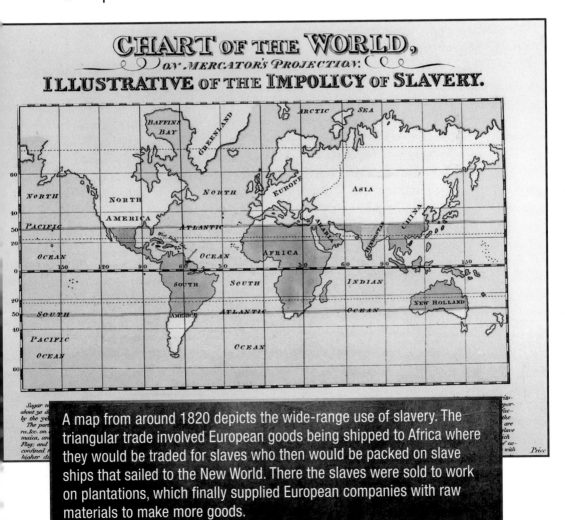

A map from around 1820 depicts the wide-range use of slavery. The triangular trade involved European goods being shipped to Africa where they would be traded for slaves who then would be packed on slave ships that sailed to the New World. There the slaves were sold to work on plantations, which finally supplied European companies with raw materials to make more goods.

The first stage began in Europe, where manufactured goods such as metals, cloth, guns, and spirits were loaded onto ships bound for ports on the African coast. There the goods were exchanged for slaves. Many slaves were taken from the region bordering the Gulf of Guinea; in fact, a section of the African coast in what are now the countries of Togo, Benin, and Nigeria became known as the Slave Coast. Many more slaves were taken from west-central Africa, centered on the Portuguese colony in what is now Angola. A smaller number came from Portuguese-controlled parts of southeastern Africa.

The second stage of the triangular trade was the shipment of slaves across the Atlantic Ocean, usually to Brazil or to an island in the Caribbean Sea. This trip, known as the Middle Passage, took a few weeks to several months. The ships were grossly overcrowded, with the captives wedged below decks and chained to platforms stacked in tiers. The average space allotted to an individual was just 6 feet long, 16 inches wide, and perhaps 3 feet high (183 by 41 by 91 centimeters). Unable to stand up or turn over, many captives died in this prone position. The almost continuous dangers faced by the captives included epidemic diseases, raids at port by hostile tribes, and attack by pirates, in addition to physical, sexual, and

Africans aboard a slave ship during the Middle Passage were subjected to horrific conditions, including overcrowding, shackles, and physical and emotional abuse.

psychological abuse at the hands of their captors. Death rates on the Middle Passage ranged from about 10 to more than 20 percent. The ship captains were paid only for slaves delivered alive.

After arriving in Brazil or the Caribbean, the slaves were sold at auction and were taken throughout the New World. The slave auctions were elaborate markets in which the prices of the slaves were determined. The auctions told the captains and their superiors what kind of cargo was in demand, usually adult males. Credit almost always was part of the transaction, and inability to collect was one of the major reasons companies went bankrupt. After the auction the slave was delivered to the new owner, who then put him to work. That also began the period of "seasoning" for the slave, the period of about a year or so when he either succumbed to the disease environment of the New World or survived it. Many slaves who landed on the North American mainland before the early 18th century had already survived the seasoning process in the Caribbean. Then they were put to work on plantations.

The shipment to Europe of plantation crops and products made from them was the third leg of the triangular trade. Among the most valuable exports to Europe were sugar, tobacco, cotton, molasses, and rum.

The peak of the Atlantic slave trade seems to have been reached in the 1780s, when on average some 78,000 slaves were brought to the Americas each year.

CHAPTER TWO

AFRICAN SLAVES IN THE AMERICAS

It was plantation, or agricultural, slavery that was established in the West Indies, Central and South America, and the British colonies of North America. A minority of slaves worked in towns or cities at trades. Most lived on plantations, where they did all the work as both house servants and fieldworkers.

The uninterrupted history of blacks in the United States began in 1619, when 20 Africans were landed in the English colony of Virginia. These blacks were not slaves but indentured servants, as were many of the white settlers. By the 1660s large numbers of Africans were being brought to the English colonies. In 1790 blacks numbered almost 760,000 and made up nearly one-fifth of the population of the United States.

Slaves prepare tobacco on a plantation in Virginia around 1790. The demand for slave labor in America grew quickly as the plantation system in the South became entrenched.

Attempts to hold servants beyond the normal term of indenture culminated in the legal establishment of black slavery in Virginia in 1661 and in all the English colonies by 1750. The blacks were easily distinguished by their color from the rest of the population, making them highly visible targets for enslavement. Moreover, the belief that they were an "inferior race" with a "heathen" culture made it easier for whites to rationalize black slavery.

Hot, humid, and blessed with a long growing season and a variety of soils, the South from its beginnings was marked for agriculture. In Virginia and North Carolina tobacco became the chief crop. In the Sea Islands off the coast of South Carolina and Georgia, rice and indigo were planted. The English and Scots-Irish settlers who had been granted large estates developed the so-called plantation system of land tenure. Because the labor requirements on plantations were great, blacks were imported from Africa and the West Indies to work the fields. Thus the cornerstones of Southern culture and land use—an agricultural base, a white population that stemmed largely from the British Isles and was overwhelmingly Protestant, the plantation system, and a black population that served as slaves—were laid early.

THE HOMELAND OF AMERICA'S SLAVES

Of an estimated 10 million Africans brought to the Americas by the slave trade, about 430,000 came to the territory of what is now the United States. The overwhelming majority of Africans were taken from the area of western Africa stretching from present-day Senegal to Angola, where political and social organization as well as art, music, and dance were highly advanced. On or near the African coast had emerged the major kingdoms of Oyo, Ashanti, Benin, Dahomey, and Kongo. In the Sudanese interior had arisen the empires of Ghana, Mali, and Songhai; the Hausa states; and Kanem-Bornu. Such African cities as Djenné and Timbuktu, both now in Mali, were at one time major commercial and educational centers.

THE CHARACTERISTICS OF SLAVERY

The two basic types of slavery are household, or domestic, slavery, and productive slavery. Domestic slaves' primary function was to serve their owners in their homes or wherever else the owners might be, such as in military service. Drawing water, hewing wood, cleaning, cooking, waiting on table, taking out the garbage, shopping, child-tending, and similar domestic occupations were the major functions of domestic slaves. Productive slaves predominantly produced marketable

A domestic slave announces a visitor to the master. A social hierarchy emerged in the plantation system: The house or domestic slaves were at the top, then came skilled craftsmen, and last were the field hands or agricultural slaves.

products in mines or on tobacco, indigo, sugar, or cotton plantations.

There was a legal relationship between slave owners. There were provisions for the recovery of runaways, and most imposed sanctions on owners who stole others' slaves or helped them to flee. There also were relatively uniform laws about passing slaves from one generation to another. Regarding the law of slave transactions, the legal system in Louisiana allowed guarantees by the sellers that slaves would not flee, were free from disease, or had certain skills.

In North America in the period from 1770 to 1830 the killing of a slave was equated in common law with the murder of a white person. Laws were uniformly harsh when a slave killed a stranger who was a freeman. Society in the American South explicitly stated that slaves could have no honor, personal status, or prestige.

SLAVE CODES

Laws known as the slave codes regulated the slave system to promote absolute control by the master and complete submission by the slave. Under these laws the slave was a piece of property and a source of labor that could be bought and sold like an animal. The slave was allowed no stable family life and little privacy. A slave was prohibited by law from learning to read or write. The meek slave received tokens of favor from the master; the rebellious slave provoked brutal punishment. A social hierarchy among the plantation slaves helped keep them divided. At the top were the house slaves; next in rank were the skilled artisans; and at the bottom were the vast majority of field hands, who bore the brunt of the harsh plantation life.

Inherent in the institution of slavery were certain social controls, which slave owners amplified with laws to protect not only the property but also the property owner from the danger of slave violence. The slave

At slave auctions, which were held in the North and South before the Civil War, slave families were often separated and sold to slaveholders in distant states.

codes were forerunners of the black codes of the mid-19th century.

In the British possessions in the New World, the settlers were free to promote any regulations they saw fit to govern their labor supply. As early as the 17th century, a set of rules was in effect in Virginia and elsewhere; but the slave codes were constantly being altered to adapt to new needs, and they varied from one colony—and, later, one state—to another.

All the slave codes, however, had certain provisions in common. In all of them the color line was firmly drawn, and any amount of African heritage established the race of a person as black, with little regard as to whether the person was slave or free. The status of the offspring followed that of the mother, so that the child of a free father and a slave mother was a slave. Slaves had few legal rights: in court their testimony was inadmissible in any litigation involving whites; they could make no contract, nor could they own property; even if attacked, they could not strike a white person. There were numerous restrictions to enforce social control: slaves could not be away from their owner's premises without permission; they could not assemble unless a white person was present; they could not own firearms; they could not be taught to read or write, nor could they transmit or possess "inflammatory" literature; they were not permitted to marry.

Obedience to the slave codes was exacted in a variety of ways. Such punishments as whipping, branding, and imprisonment were commonly used. Some slaves, especially those who committed violence against whites, were killed, although slaves' value to their owners as labor discouraged the practice.

RAID OF SECON

[A TYPICAL N

We publish herewith three p tographs by M'Pherson and O Gordon, who escaped from his sippi, and came into our lines March last. One of these port man as he entered our lines, wit covered with mud and dirt fr through the swamps and bayou been for days and nights by hi eral neighbors and a pack of blo er shows him as he underwent ination previous to being muste —his back furrowed and scarre of a whipping administered last; and the third represents hi uniform, bearing the musket duty.

This negro displayed unusua energy. In order to foil the hounds who were chasing him plantation onions, which he carr After crossing each creek or sw body freely with these onions, frequently threw the dogs off th At one time in Louisiana he

GORDON AS HE ENTEREI

...LINA VOLUNTEERS (COL. MONTGOMERY) AMONG THE RICE PLANTATIONS ON THE COMBAHEE, S. C.—[See Page 427.]

as guide, and on one expedition was unfortunately taken prisoner by the rebels, who, infuriated beyond measure, tied him up and beat him, leaving him for dead. He came to life, however, and once more made his escape to our lines.

By way of illustrating the degree of brutality which slavery has developed among the whites in the section of country from which this negro came, we append the following extract from a letter in the New York *Times*, recounting what was told by

the refugees from Mrs. GILLESPIE's estate on the Black River:

The treatment of the slaves, they say, has been growing worse and worse for the last six or seven years.

Flogging with a leather strap on the naked body is common; also, paddling the body with a hand-saw until the skin is a mass of blisters, and then breaking the blisters with the teeth of the saw. They have "very often" seen slaves stretched out upon the ground with hands and feet held down by fellow-slaves, or lashed to stakes driven into the ground for "burning." Handfuls of dry corn-husks are then lighted, and the burning embers are whipped off with a stick so as to fall in showers of live sparks upon the naked back. This is continued until the victim is covered with blisters. If in his writhings of torture the slave gets his hands free to brush off the fire, the burning brand is applied to them.

Another method of punishment, which is inflicted for the higher order of crimes, such as running away, or other refractory conduct, is to dig a hole in the ground large enough for the slave to squat or lie down in. The victim is then stripped naked and placed in the hole, and a covering or grating of green sticks is laid over the opening. Upon this a quick fire is built, and the live embers sifted through upon the naked flesh of the slave, until his body is blistered and swollen almost to bursting. With just enough of life to enable him to crawl, the slave is then allowed to recover from his wounds if he can, or to end his sufferings by death.

"Charley Sloo" and "Overton," two hands, were both murdered by these cruel tortures. "Sloo" was whipped to death, dying under the infliction, or soon after punishment. "Overton" was laid naked upon his face and burned as above described, so that the cords of his legs and the

GORDON UNDER MEDICAL INSPECTION.

GORDON IN HIS UNIFORM AS A U. S. SOLDIER.

An 1863 *Harper's Weekly* article about the runaway slave named Gordon who joined the Union army includes an engraving of his bare back that shows the scars from being whipped while a slave in Mississippi.

AMERICAN INDEPENDENCE

Crispus Attucks, a former slave killed in the Boston Massacre of 1770, was the first martyr to the cause

Crispus Attucks, the First Martyr of the American King (now State) Street, Boston, March 5th, 1770.

The former slave Crispus Attucks was the first victim to fall in the Boston Massacre and gained notoriety as one of the first people to die for the cause of American independence from Great Britain.

ition,
e 16.

of American independence from Great Britain. During the American Revolution (1775–1781), some 5,000 black soldiers and sailors fought on the American side. After the Revolution, some slaves—particularly former soldiers—were freed, and the Northern states abolished slavery. But with the ratification of the United States Constitution, in 1788, slavery became more firmly entrenched than ever in the South. The Constitution counted a slave as three-fifths of a person for purposes of taxation and representation in Congress, extended the African slave trade for 20 years, and provided for the return of fugitive slaves to their owners.

THE PARADOX OF THE FOUNDING FATHERS

The most prominent American statesmen during the American Revolution and the formation of the United States are known as the country's

THOMAS JEFFERSON AND THE ISSUE OF SLAVERY

Thomas Jefferson's position on slavery was complex. In his only book, *Notes on the State of Virginia* (1781), Jefferson discussed how slavery violated human rights and contradicted the principles of freedom and equality upon which the United States was founded. He blamed slavery on the aristocratic society created by Great Britain in the colonies. His proposals in the Continental Congress during the 1780s were aimed at gradually abolishing slavery, starting with new U.S. territories and newborn slaves. These statements and actions put Jefferson at the forefront of the antislavery movement.

The Continental Congress sent Jefferson to Paris in 1784 (two years after Jefferson's wife, Martha, had died) to succeed Benjamin Franklin as U.S. ambassador to France. Jefferson's daughter Patsy went with him to Paris in 1784, and he sent for his daughter Polly, accompanied by his mulatto slave Sally Hemings, in 1787 to join them. The most controversial segment of Jefferson's personal life was his alleged love affair with Hemings. Historians speculated that the affair began after Hemings arrived in Paris. Scholars estimated that he fathered at least one and possibly six of Hemings's children. Research continued, and in 1998 scientists conducted a DNA analysis on some of Jefferson's and Hemings' living descendants. The tests showed that it was almost certain that Jefferson and Hemings had had children together. Nevertheless, their romance remains a topic of debate.

By the time he returned to the United States in 1789, however, Jefferson's antislavery position had generated controversy. It was clear that Jefferson's position was inconsistent. Alongside his antislavery arguments in *Notes on the State of Virginia*, he also asserted that people of African descent were biologically inferior to whites. He believed that blacks and whites could never coexist peacefully, therefore making the ending of slavery inconceivable. Jefferson's dependence on slave labor at Monticello, his home in Virginia, gave his critics another reason to describe his antislavery rhetoric as hypocritical.

Founding Fathers. These men were responsible for leading the war that won the American colonies independence from Great Britain. They are also responsible for the shape the new country took. Founding Fathers wrote and approved the Declaration of Independence, which emphasizes the importance of protecting the freedom of individuals. They were also responsible for the creation of the Constitution, which established the new country as a republic, or a democracy with representative government.

Among the men almost always included on any list of the Founding Fathers are John Adams, Samuel Adams, Benjamin Franklin, Alexander Hamilton, Patrick Henry, Thomas Jefferson, James Madison, John Marshall, George Mason, and George Washington. Although the achievements of the Founding Fathers are great—they held the democratic principle that political power in the government should belong to the citizens, for example—scholars emphasize their failures in two major areas, the failure to end slavery and the failure to establish a fair policy toward Native Americans.

Slavery was incompatible with the values of the American Revolution, and all the prominent members of the Revolutionary generation acknowledged that fact. The Founders ended the further importation of slaves from

Africa in 1808. They also made slavery illegal in the North and the Northwest Territory (now part of the Midwest). However, they failed to abolish the domestic slave trade in the South, where the economy was growing more dependent on slavery. They eventually insisted that the legality of slavery was a matter for the individual states to decide, not the national government. This position permitted the slave population to grow greatly in size.

There were at least three reasons for this tragic failure. First, many Founders mistakenly believed that slavery would die out on its own, because it would not be as advantageous as using free labor. They did not foresee, however, that the invention of the cotton gin in 1793 would make growing cotton with slave labor highly profitable. Second, all the early efforts of the Founding Fathers to make slavery a national issue were met with the threat that some Southern states would secede. The new country was still in a fragile phase, and the Founders believed it would not have been able to survive the loss of these states. Finally, even though the Founders opposed slavery in principle, many had deep-seated racial prejudice against blacks. Like most white Americans of the time, they could not envision a United States where both blacks and whites could live together as free people. Many of the Founding Fathers were themselves slave owners.

CHAPTER THREE

KING COTTON AND THE EXPANSION OF SLAVERY

Following Eli Whitney's invention of the cotton gin in 1793—an innovation that made the production of cotton far easier and less expensive—cotton growing on a large scale spread widely and became yet another cornerstone in Southern culture and land use. By 1800 cotton production had increased from about 3,000 bales a year to 73,000. To supply the growing demands of mill owners in England and New England, planters imported more slaves to work the cotton fields. The number of slaves soared from about

Slaves work an early cotton gin in the 1860s. Eli Whitney's cotton-cleaning invention brought prosperity to the South because it made the production of cotton easier and cotton's sale price lower. The South grew cotton on a much larger scale after the gin's invention.

700,000 in 1793 to nearly 4,000,000 by 1860. Plantations sprang up in Alabama, Mississippi, Missouri, Louisiana, Tennessee, and Arkansas.

Cotton could be grown profitably on smaller plots than could sugar, with the result that in 1860 the average cotton plantation had only about 35 slaves, not all of whom produced cotton. During the reign of "King Cotton," about 40 percent of the Southern population consisted of black slaves. Whitney's cotton-cleaning invention brought prosperity to the South, but it also

Cotton helped to produce a wealthy plantation society in the South. Black slaves formed a majority of the population in many agricultural areas. In the Delta region of Mississippi, for example, black slaves outnumbered the white population ten to one.

facilitated the spread of slavery. Although Northern businessmen made great fortunes from the slave trade and from investments in Southern plantations, slavery was never widespread in the North.

This print of an imploring male slave in chains appeared on an 1837 broadside publication of John Greenleaf Whittier's antislavery poem "Our Countrymen in Chains." The image was first adopted as the seal of the Society for the Abolition of Slavery in England in the 1780s.

THE END OF THE SLAVE TRADE AND RISE OF SLAVE LABOR

Although the states of the North abolished, or ended, slavery between 1777 and 1804, it remained legal in the South. A provision in the Constitution, which was written in 1787, prohibited Congress from abolishing the slave trade for 20 years. The slave trade was finally banned in the United States in 1807 and took effect on January 1, 1808, but widespread smuggling of slaves continued until about 1862. The official end of the African slave trade in 1808 spurred the growth of the domestic slave trade in the United States, especially as a source of labor for the new cotton lands in the Southern interior. Increasingly, the supply of slaves came to be supplemented by the practice of "slave breeding," in which women slaves were encouraged—or forced—to conceive as early as 13 years of age and to give birth as often as possible.

THE MISSOURI COMPROMISE

The Missouri Compromise solved a problem that had been brewing in the United States over the issue of slavery. It allowed Missouri to enter the Union as a state where slavery was permitted, while banning slavery in certain other places. Passed by the U.S Congress in 1820, it marked the beginning of the conflict over the spread of slavery that led to the American Civil War.

In 1818 the Missouri territory applied for statehood. At that time there were 11 free states and 11 slave states in the Union. Slavery had been practiced

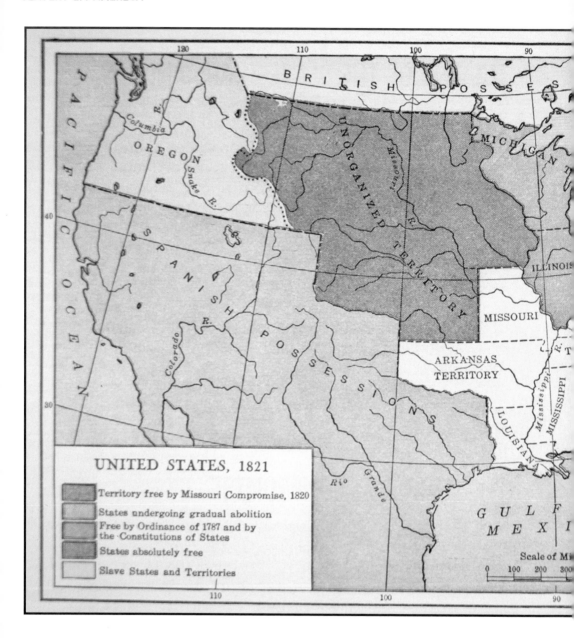

UNITED STATES, 1821

Territory free by Missouri Compromise, 1820

States undergoing gradual abolition

Free by Ordinance of 1787 and by the Constitutions of States

States absolutely free

Slave States and Territories

This 1821 map shows the slave and free states and territories of the United States after the Missouri Compromise of 1820.

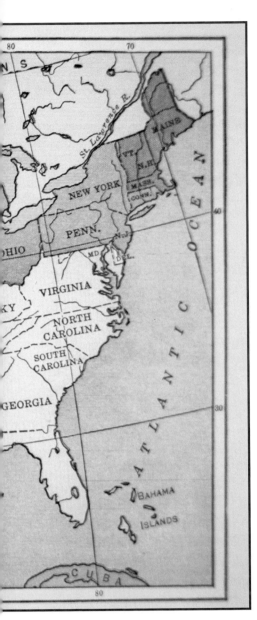

in Missouri for many years. The admission of Missouri would therefore upset the balance of states. The U.S. Congress could not agree on whether to allow Missouri to join the Union.

Finally, late in 1819 Maine also applied for admission to the Union, and a way was seen to maintain the balance of power. Representative Henry Clay of Kentucky, who came to be called the Great Compromiser, came up with the plan. The lawmakers agreed that Maine would be admitted as a free state and Missouri as a slave state. In addition, Missouri's southern border would mark the northern limit of where slavery would be allowed in any other new state. The compromise temporarily stopped the debate.

CHAPTER FOUR

SLAVE REBELLIONS

Throughout history humans have objected to being enslaved and have responded in myriad ways. The most dramatic form of slave protest was outright rebellion. Slave uprisings varied enormously in frequency, size, intensity, and duration. Slave rebellions in North America were noticeably few and involved only a handful of participants: the New York revolt of 1712, the Stono rebellion of South Carolina (1739), the Gabriel Prosser plot in Richmond, Virginia (1800), the Denmark Vesey conspiracy in Charleston, South Carolina (1822), and Nat Turner's uprising in Jerusalem, Virginia (1831), are the best known. Southern slave uprisings were so few and so small because of the absolute

A monument to Denmark Vesey, a former slave who had bought his freedom and who planned a slave revolt, is located in Hampton Park in Charleston, South Carolina.

certainty that they would be brutally repressed. The Turner rebellion is usually given as the reason for the marked increase in the severity of the slave regime after 1831.

NAT TURNER

The most effective slave revolt in United States history was led by a young black man, Nat Turner (1800–31), who regarded himself as an agent of God to lead his people out of bondage. The revolt ended the false belief that slaves were either happy with their lives as they were or were too submissive to rebel.

Turner was born on a small plantation in Southampton County, Virginia. In the relatively easygoing atmosphere at this particular plantation, he was allowed to learn to read and write, and he hungrily absorbed much religious instruction as well. In the early 1820s he was sold to a nearby farmer and again in 1831 to a craftsman named Joseph Travis.

Nat Turner and his companions are depicted in a wooden area of the Dismal Swamp in Virginia in 1831. Turner insisted that God gave him a sign to launch the rebellion, which was finally put down by the Virginia state militia.

By this time his religion had become fanaticism. An eclipse of the sun in 1831 made him believe the time for insurrection had come. He planned to capture the armory at Jerusalem, the county seat. On August 21, with six other slaves, he killed the Travis family. Nearly 60 slaves rallied to his cause, and in the next two days 55 whites were murdered. The revolt was handicapped, however, by a lack of discipline among his followers and the fact that so few slaves turned out to help him. Armed resistance from whites, aided by a 3,000-member force of state militia, ended the rebellion.

Most of the slaves were killed or captured. Turner escaped capture for six weeks but was finally caught, convicted, and hanged at Jerusalem on November 11, 1831. His action subsequently set off a wave of legislation prohibiting the education, movement, and assembly of slaves. In 1832 *The Confessions of Nat Turner...as told to Thomas R. Grey* was published.

MAJOR SLAVE REVOLTS IN THE UNITED STATES

In American history, periodic acts of violent resistance by slaves during more than two centuries of slavery signified continual deep-rooted discontent with the condition of bondage and resulted in harsher mechanisms for social control and repression in slaveholding areas.

Estimates of the total number of slave revolts vary according to the definition of insurrection. For the two centuries preceding the American Civil War (1861–65), one historian found documentary evidence of more

HORRID MASSACRE IN VIRGINIA.

The Scenes which the above Plate is designed to represent, are---Figure 1. a Mother intreating for the lives of her children. ---2. Mr. Travis, cruelly murdered by his own Slaves.---3. Mr. Barrow, who bravely defended himself until his wife escaped. ----4. A company of mounted Dragoons in pursuit of the Blacks.

Just Published, an Authentic and Interesting

NARRATIVE

OF THE

TRAGICAL SCENE

Which was witnessed in Southampton county (Virginia) on Monday the 22d of August last, when FIFTY FIVE of its inhabitants (mostly women and children) were inhumanly massacred by the Blacks!

Short and imperfect sketches of the horrid massacre above mentioned have appeared in the public Journals, but the public are now presented with every particular relative thereto, communicated by those who were eye witnesses of the bloody scene, and confirmed by the confessions of several of the Blacks while under sentence of death.

A more shocking instance of human butchery has seldom occurred in any country, and never before in this—the merciless wretches carried destruction to every white person they found in the houses, whether the hoary head, the lovely virgin, or the sleeping infant in the cradle! they spared none !—a widow (Mrs. Whitehead) and her 10 children were murdered in one house ! among the slain on that fatal night, was an amiable young lady but 17 years of age, who the day following was to have been united in marriage to a young gentleman of North-Carolina, who had left home the evening preceding with the expectation of conveying there the succeeding day the object of his affections ! but, alas ! how sad was his disappointment ! he was the third person who entered the house after the horrid massacre, to witness the mangled remains of her whom he was so shortly to espouse ! The Blacks after having completed their work of death, attempted to evade the pursuit of those who had collected to oppose them, by secreting themselves in a neighboring swamp, to the borders of which they were pursued by a company of mounted dragoons. Of the fifty five slain nearly two thirds of the number were children, not exceeding twelve years of age ! and it was truly a melancholly scene (as was observed to the writer by one who witnessed it) to behold on the day of their interment so great a number of coffins collected, surrounded by the weeping relatives !

While the friends of humanity however or wherever situated. cannot but sincerely and deeply lament the awful destruction of so many innocent lives, yet, the humane and philanthopic citizens of New-England, and of the middle States, cannot feel too thankful for the repose and peace of conscience which they enjoy, by wisely and humanely abolishing laws dooming a free born fellow being (without fault or crime) to perpetual bondage !—an example truly worthy of imitation by our brethren at the South.

The Narrative (which contains every important particular relating to the horrid massacre) is afforded for the trifling sum of 12 1-2 Cents. ☞ This paper left for perusal, and to be returned when called for.

An engraving depicts the Nat Turner slave rebellion in which at least 55 whites were murdered. The revolt resulted in new harsh laws prohibiting the education, movement, and assembly of slaves.

than 250 uprisings or attempted uprisings involving 10 or more slaves whose aim was personal freedom. Few of these, however, were systematically planned, and most were merely spontaneous and quite short-lived disturbances by small groups of slaves. Such rebellions were usually attempted by male bondsmen and were often betrayed by house servants who identified more closely with their masters.

Three rebellions or attempted rebellions by slaves do deserve special notice, however. The first large-scale conspiracy was conceived by blacksmith Gabriel Prosser in the summer of 1800. On August 30 more than 1,000 armed slaves massed for action near Richmond, Virginia, but were thwarted by a violent rainstorm. The slaves were forced to disband, and 35 were hanged, including Prosser.

The only free person to lead a rebellion was Denmark Vesey, an urban artisan of Charleston, South Carolina. Vesey's rebellion (1822) was to have involved, according to some accounts, as many as 9,000 slaves from the surrounding area, but the conspiracy was betrayed in June before the plan could be carried out. As a result 139 blacks were arrested, of whom 37 (including Vesey) were hanged and 32 exiled before the end of the summer.

The third notable slave rebellion was led by Nat Turner, in Southampton County, Virginia, in the summer of 1831. On the evening of August 21 a band of seven slaves started their crusade against bondage, killing a total of 55 whites and attracting about 60 fellow slaves to the conspiracy during the next few days. On the 24th, hundreds of militia and volunteers stopped the rebels near Jerusalem, the county seat, killing more than 50. Turner was later hanged.

Death of Capt. Ferrer, the Cap

Don Jose Ruiz and Don Pedro Montez, of the Island of Cuba, having pu
on board the Amistad, Capt. Ferrer, in order to transport them to Principe
four days, the African captives on board, in order to obtain their freedom,
Captain and crew of the vessel. Capt. Ferrer and the cook of the vessel w

A successful revolt by Africans, led by Joseph Cinque, occurred in 1839 on the slave ship *Amistad*. When the vessel reached Long Island, New York, the Africans went ashore and were charged with murder and mutiny. Their case reached the U.S. Supreme Court, whereby the Africans regained their freedom and were returned to Africa.

A new wave of unrest spread through the South, accompanied by corresponding fear among slaveholders and passage of more repressive legislation directed against both slaves and free blacks. These measures were aimed particularly at restricting the education of blacks, their freedom of movement and assembly, and the circulation of inflammatory printed material.

Although the slave rebellion known as the *Amistad* mutiny occurred on a slave ship off the coast of Cuba

f the Amistad, July, 1839.

y-three slaves at Havana, recently imported from Africa, put them
rt on the Island of Cuba. After being out from Havana about
o Africa, armed themselves with cane knives, and rose upon the
two of the crew escaped; Ruiz and Montez were made prisoners.

in the summer of 1839, the 53 African captives who revolted were captured and tried in the United States after their ship entered U.S. waters. Their legal victory in 1840 in a federal court in Connecticut, where slavery was still legal due to gradual abolition, was upheld by the U.S. Supreme Court in the following year. With help from abolitionist and missionary groups, the Africans returned home to Sierra Leone in 1842.

In the decades preceding the American Civil War, increasing numbers of discontented slaves escaped to the North or to Canada via the Underground Railroad. Publicity in the North concerning black rebellions and the influx of fugitive slaves helped to arouse wider sympathy for the plight of the slave and support for the abolition movement.

CHAPTER FIVE

THE ABOLITIONIST MOVEMENT AND THE WAR BETWEEN THE STATES

Between 1800 and 1830 the antislavery movement in the North looked for ways to eventually eliminate slavery from the United States. One popular plan was to colonize Liberia, in Africa, as a refuge for former black slaves. The American Colonization Society began settling freed slaves and freeborn blacks there in the 1820s.

More and more Northerners became convinced that slavery should not be allowed to spread to new territories. At the same time Southerners were becoming equally determined to create new slave states. The slave states had long been a separate section economically. Now they began to regard themselves as a separate social and political unit as well.

FREDERICK DOUGLASS

Frederick Douglass (1818?–95) became one of the foremost black abolitionists and civil rights leaders in the United States. He was born Frederick Augustus Washington Bailey in Talbot County, Maryland. His father was an unknown white man; his mother, Harriet Bailey, was a slave. He was separated from her and raised by her elderly parents.

In 1838 Frederick escaped to New York City, where he lived as a free man. On September 15, 1838, he married Anna Murray of Baltimore, a free woman. They settled in New Bedford, Massachusetts, and Frederick changed his last name to Douglass.

Douglass read the *Liberator*, an antislavery newspaper published by the white abolitionist William Lloyd Garrison. In 1841 at an antislavery convention, Douglass described his slave life in a moving speech that began his career as an abolitionist. He became an agent of the Massachusetts Anti-Slavery Society and in this capacity lectured to large assemblies. Many listeners were so impressed by Douglass's appearance and personality that they could not believe he had ever been a slave. He had never revealed his former name or the name of his master. To dispel doubts about his past, he published an autobiography in 1845, *The Narrative*

(continued on the next page)

(continued from the previous page)

of the Life of Frederick Douglass: An American Slave. Fearful that it might lead to his re-enslavement, Douglass fled to Great Britain. English Quakers raised money to purchase his freedom, and in 1847 he returned home, now legally free.

This daguerreotype portrait of Frederick Douglass was taken around 1850. Douglass helped abolitionist Gerrit Smith organize the 1850 Anti-Fugitive Slave Law Convention in Cazenovia, New York, to establish ways to fight the proposed Fugitive Slave Act.

That year, Douglass founded a new antislavery newspaper, the *North Star*—later renamed *Frederick Douglass's Paper*—in Rochester, New York. Unlike Garrison, he had come to believe that political action rather than moral persuasion would bring about the abolition of slavery. By 1853, he had broken with Garrison and become a strong and independent abolitionist.

When the American Civil War began, in 1861, Douglass urged that it be fought to abolish slavery. He applauded President Abraham Lincoln's final Emancipation Proclamation of 1863, which freed slaves in the rebellious states, but expressed his disappointment that not all slaves had been freed.

THE WORK OF THE ABOLITIONISTS

After Congress passed the Missouri Compromise of 1820, an uneasy peace was preserved for almost a generation. While many abolitionists were working for the gradual abolishment of slavery, a much more strident form of abolitionism emerged in the 1830s. It called for the immediate outlawing of slavery. The most notable leader of this movement was William Lloyd Garrison. On January 1, 1831, he published the first issue of his newspaper, the *Liberator*, calling for the immediate emancipation, or freeing, of all slaves in the United States. This was the most extreme of abolitionist positions, and it never gained a large following in the North. But the zeal with which Garrison and his associates pursued their cause gave them a great deal of both influence and notoriety.

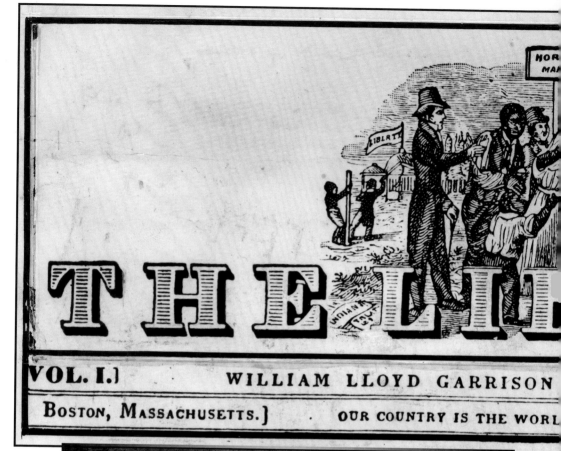

VOL. I.]   WILLIAM LLOYD GARRISON

BOSTON, MASSACHUSETTS.]   ·   OUR COUNTRY IS THE WORL

The 1831 masthead of the antislavery weekly the *Liberator*, published by William Lloyd Garrison and Isaac Knapp, illustrates a slave auction with the sign "Slaves, Horses, and Other Cattle to be Sold." The caption under the masthead reads "Our Country Is the World—Our Countrymen Are Mankind."

Garrison founded the American Anti-Slavery Society in 1833. For some 30 years this organization was a powerful but divisive influence in the United States. It never had the support of a majority of Northerners. Most did not like what they saw as its extremism; they were aware that the U.S. Constitution left it to the states to decide about slavery, and they did not want

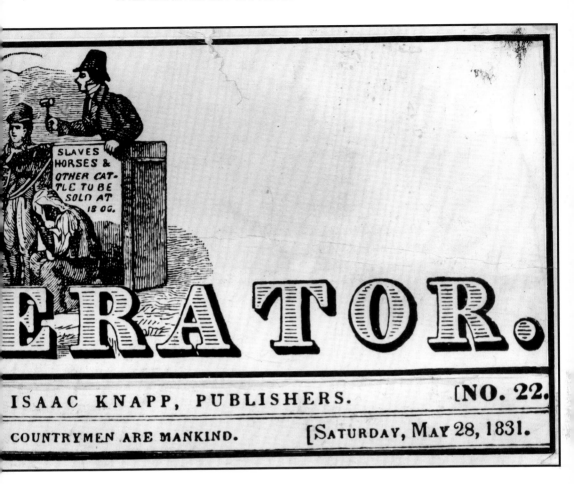

SLAVES HORSES & OTHER CAT-TLE TO BE SOLD AT 18 OG.

ERATOR.

ISAAC KNAPP, PUBLISHERS.

[NO. 22.

COUNTRYMEN ARE MANKIND.

[SATURDAY, MAY 28, 1831.

to see the union divided. And even though the Northern states had abolished slavery, Northern whites did not want a large black population living in their midst.

Other abolitionists included clergymen and people active in religious communities such as Theodore Dwight Weld and Theodore Parker. Literary figures such as John Greenleaf Whittier, James Russell Lowell, and Lydia Maria Child also joined the movement. Free blacks, particularly former slaves Frederick Douglass and William Wells Brown, were eloquent speakers for the cause.

HEAVY WEIGHTS—ARRIVAL OF A PARTY AT LEA

(Fifteen escaped in this Schooner.)

Escaped slaves from Virginia arrive at League Island, Pennsylvania, in 1856, and are helped by the Underground Railroad. This picture appeared in African American abolitionist William Still's book about the Underground Railroad, which was published in 1872. Still was a valiant conductor of the Underground Railroad in Pennsylvania.

THE UNDERGROUND RAILROAD

For more than four decades before the American Civil War, there existed an organized system in the Northern states established to help escaped slaves reach places of safety in the North and in Canada. This system was called the Underground Railroad because its activities were carried on in secret and because railway terms were used to describe the system in order to disguise the real nature of the operation.

Once in Canada slaves were free from the prosecution mandated by the Fugitive Slave Acts. These statutes, passed by Congress in 1793 and 1850, provided for the capture and return of slaves who escaped into free states or territories. To counteract these laws, personal-liberty laws were passed by some Northern states. Although these personal-liberty laws could not make slaves free, they did hamper federal officials and judges in implementing the Fugitive Slave Acts.

This 1870 illustration from Harriet Beecher Stowe's book *Uncle Tom's Cabin* (originally published in 1852) depicts the death of Uncle Tom after he was beaten by Simon Legree, Sambo, and Quimbo. Eva watches from heaven, waiting for Uncle Tom to join her. Stowe's book had a significant impact on how the public viewed slavery and its effect on families.

The Underground Railroad extended throughout 14 Northern states from Maine to Nebraska, but its heaviest activities were concentrated in Pennsylvania, Ohio, Indiana, New York, and the New England states. The freed slaves were called "freight," routes were called "lines," stopping places were "stations," and those who helped the slaves along the way were "conductors." Slaves were helped from one transfer place to another until they reached Canada. Hundreds of slaves avoided the overland journey by traveling to New England as stowaways on ships from Southern ports. From New England they made their way to New Brunswick.

Those who were most active in helping slaves to escape by way of the "railroad" were Northern abolitionists and other antislavery groups, including members of several Protestant denominations, especially Quakers, Methodists, and Mennonites. The Quaker leader Thomas Garrett is reputed to have helped about 2,700 slaves escape to freedom. Some former slaves were also active in the system. One of these was Harriet Tubman. Harriet Beecher Stowe, author of the novel *Uncle Tom's Cabin* (1852), which described the horrors slaves faced and which many people believed helped bring about the Civil War, found out that her servant in Cincinnati, Ohio, was a runaway slave. Stowe and her husband helped the servant escape through the Underground Railroad. Estimates of the total number of slaves who reached freedom by way of the Underground Railroad vary between 40,000 and 100,000. When the Civil War started in 1861, the railroad's activities ceased.

HARRIET TUBMAN

A runaway slave herself, Harriet Tubman helped so many blacks escape to freedom that she became known as the "Moses of her people."

Harriet Tubman was born Araminta Ross about 1820 on a plantation near Bucktown, Maryland. She was one of 11 children of a slave couple. At seven she was hired out to do housework and to care for white children. Later she became a field hand. While still a teenager, she was struck on the head by an overseer. As a result of the blow, she fell asleep suddenly several times each day for the rest of her life. Hard work toughened her, and before she was 19 she was as strong as the men with whom she worked.

In 1844 Ross married a free black, John Tubman. She left him in 1849, when her fear of being sold farther south spurred her to escape. She traveled at night, aided by the Underground Railroad.

In Pennsylvania and New Jersey, Tubman worked as a maid. By December 1850 she had saved enough money to make the first of 19 daring journeys back into the South to lead other slaves out of bondage. In 1851 she returned for her husband but found he had remarried.

Tubman worked closely with the Underground Railroad. She maintained strict discipline during the perilous journeys to the North. If a runaway lagged behind or lost faith and wished to

(continued on the next page)

Harriet Tubman, called the "Moses of her people," became well known as a conductor on the Underground Railroad. She helped her family and hundreds of other fugitive slaves to freedom.

(continued from the previous page)

turn back, she forced him on at gunpoint. Before the Civil War she freed her parents and most of her brothers and sisters as well as hundreds of other slaves. Much later in life she proudly recalled: "I never ran my train off the track, and I never lost a passenger."

During the Civil War Tubman served the Union Army. She nursed and cooked for white soldiers, and for sick and starving blacks who sought protection behind Union lines. She acted as both a scout and a spy, often bravely leading Union raiding parties into Confederate territory.

Harriet Tubman died in Auburn, New York, on March 10, 1913, and was buried with military honors.

THE REPEAL OF THE MISSOURI COMPROMISE, THE DRED SCOTT DECISION, AND THE RAID AT HARPERS FERRY

The conflict over slavery was renewed when Senator Stephen A. Douglas of Illinois persuaded Congress to repeal the Missouri Compromise in 1854. His new measure, the Kansas-Nebraska Act, allowed the people of Kansas and Nebraska to decide for themselves if their territories would allow slavery. The act led to the first armed conflict between North and South. The tension between the two regions was later heightened by the Dred Scott decision.

The controversial 1857 ruling of the U.S. Supreme Court in the case of Dred Scott made slavery legal in all the territories. Dred Scott was a black slave who belonged to an officer in the United States Army. His master had taken him from the slave state of Missouri to the free state of Illinois and then to Wisconsin Territory, which had been declared a free territory by the Missouri Compromise of 1820. When his master was ordered back to Missouri by the Army, Scott went with him. After his master died, however, Scott sued, claiming that he was no longer a slave because he had lived on free soil. The case was carried to the United States Supreme Court. On March 6, 1857, a majority of the court declared that Scott was still a slave and not a citizen and so had no constitutional right to sue in a federal court. The decision further held that Congress had no power to prohibit slavery in the territories and that the Missouri Compromise therefore was unconstitutional.

In the North and West many people now began to accept the fact that slavery was morally wrong and that a start should be made toward its extinction. However, some abolitionists wanted direct action. In 1859, the United States was jolted by the actions of the militant abolitionist John Brown, who believed that violence was the only way left to free the slaves. Brown led a raid on a federal arsenal in Harpers Ferry, Virginia (now in West Virginia), in an attempt to get weapons to arm blacks for a rebellion in the South. Although the raid was unsuccessful, Southern slaveholders became convinced that abolitionists would stop at nothing to eradicate slavery.

THE CIVIL WAR AND THE EMANCIPATION PROCLAMATION

Meanwhile, a new political party, the Republican Party, had been formed in 1854 to combat the extension of slavery. This party gained strength so rapidly that Southern leaders threatened to secede from the Union if the "Black Republicans" came to power. When the new party did win the elections of 1860, Abraham Lincoln was chosen president. Lincoln was not an abolitionist, but he was opposed to the spread of slavery into the West.

Many people in the South felt that their entire way of life was greatly threatened by Lincoln's election. As a result, the Southern states carried out their threat. They were led by South Carolina, which withdrew from the Union on December 20, 1860. By February 1861, six other states of the lower South—Mississippi, Florida, Alabama, Georgia, Louisiana, and Texas—had seceded. The states that seceded set up a new government, the Confederate States of America, or the Confederacy, and made Jefferson Davis president.

In September 1862, President Lincoln issued a proclamation that he later called "the central act of my administration, and the greatest event of the 19th century." This preliminary proclamation called on the seceding states to return to their allegiance before the next year, otherwise their slaves would be declared free people. The Confederate states and their slaveholders paid no attention to the warning, and so on January 1, 1863, Lincoln issued the final proclamation that freed the slaves in the Southern states.

Enfranchised slaves celebrate President Abraham Lincoln's final Emancipation Proclamation in 1863. The decree altered the Civil War from a fight to keep the Union from disintegrating to a battle for human liberty.

The Emancipation Proclamation could not be enforced in the regions held by Confederate troops, and it did not apply to the border states, which were not in rebellion against the Union. Nevertheless, the proclamation was important because it transformed the war from a struggle to preserve the Union into a crusade for human freedom. It also brought some substantial practical results by opening the Union Army to black soldiers. As soon as the Northern armies captured a region, the slaves there were given their freedom. Nearly 180,000 of the freed slaves joined the Union Army. The Civil War ended when the South surrendered in April 1865. The remaining slaves in the United States were freed by the Thirteenth Amendment to the Constitution (ratified on December 6, 1865), which decreed that "Neither slavery nor involuntary servitude, except as a punishment for crime whereof the party shall have been duly convicted, shall exist within the United States, or any place subject to their jurisdiction."

CONCLUSION

As a result of the Union victory in the Civil War and the ratification of the Thirteenth Amendment to the Constitution (1865), nearly four million black slaves were freed. The Fourteenth Amendment (1868)

In Washington, D.C., African Americans gather to commemorate the passage of the Thirteenth Amendment to the U.S. Constitution, which formally abolished slavery in the United States. The amendment was ratified on December 6, 1865.

granted blacks citizenship, and the Fifteenth Amendment (1870) guaranteed their right to vote.

During the Reconstruction period, blacks wielded political power in the South for the first time. Their leaders were largely clergymen, lawyers, and teachers who had been educated in the North and abroad. Among the ablest were Robert B. Elliott of South Carolina and John R. Lynch of Mississippi. Both were speakers of their respective state House of Representatives and were members of the U.S. Congress.

But black political power was short-lived. Northern politicians grew increasingly conciliatory to the white South, so that by 1872 virtually all leaders of the Confederacy had been pardoned and were able to vote and hold office. By means of economic pressure and the terrorist activities of violent anti-black groups, such as the Ku Klux Klan, most blacks were kept away from the polls. By 1877, with the withdrawal of the last federal troops from the South, Southern whites were again in full control. Blacks were disenfranchised, or deprived the right to vote, by the provisions of new state constitutions such as those adopted by Mississippi in 1890 and by South Carolina and Louisiana in 1895. Only a few Southern black elected officials lingered on. No black was to serve in the U.S. Congress for three decades after the departure of George H. White of North Carolina in 1901.

The rebirth of white supremacy in the South was accompanied by the growth of enforced racial separation. Starting with Tennessee in 1870, all the Southern states reenacted laws prohibiting racial intermarriage. They also passed laws, called Jim Crow laws, segregating blacks and whites in almost all public places. By 1885 most Southern states had officially segregated their public schools.

Although the Union's victory in the American Civil War and the ratification of the Thirteenth Amendment to the U.S. Constitution in 1865 brought an end to slavery in the United States, African Americans found that there still were many challenges that lay ahead of them besides the Jim Crow laws—including the sharecropper system that grew in the South during Reconstruction, the controversial "separate but equal" doctrine, disenfranchisement, and the obstacles to voting that persisted despite the passage of civil rights legislation—before they could attain true freedom.

TIMELINE

PREHISTORIC TIMES TO MODERN TIMES

Slavery exists in Africa and elsewhere.

1500S

Europeans begin transporting large numbers of Africans across the Atlantic Ocean.

1619

Twenty Africans are first brought by ship as indentured servants to the English colony of Virginia.

1661

The legal establishment of slavery takes place in the colony of Virginia.

1750

The legal establishment of slavery occurs in all English colonies in the New World.

1770

Crispus Attucks, escaped slave, becomes the first colonial soldier to die for American independence when he is killed on March 5 in the Boston Massacre.

1775-83

The American Revolution to win independence from Great Britain is fought by the 13 North American colonies.

1776

In the Declaration of Independence, a passage that condemned the slave trade is removed because of political pressure from the southern colonies.

1777-1804

All states north of Maryland abolish slavery although the process is gradual in some states, with some blacks remaining enslaved well into the nineteenth century.

1788

The U.S. Constitution is ratified and allows for the continuation of the slave trade for another 20 years. It also requires states to assist slaveholders in the recovery of fugitive slaves and specifies that a slave counts as three-fifths of a person for the purposes of taxation and for determining representation in the House of Representatives.

1793

Eli Whitney invents the cotton gin, making the growing and cleaning of cotton possible on a huge scale in the South. The increase in cotton cultivation greatly raises the demand for slaves, whose numbers rise rapidly. U.S. Congress passes the first Fugitive Slave Act, which authorizes a judge alone to decide the status of an alleged escaped slave, makes it a crime to harbor a fugitive slave, and allows slaveholders and their agents to search for escaped slaves within the borders of free states.

1800

Gabriel Prosser of Richmond, Virginia, tries to organize the first large-scale slave revolt in the United States; the plot fails and Prosser and 35 others are executed.

1807-1808

U.S. Congress bans the African slave trade in 1807, which takes effect in January 1808.

1820

Missouri Compromise is passed by Congress, allowing Missouri to become the 24th state in the Union; Maine had earlier entered the Union as a free state.

1822

Former slave Denmark Vesey plots a slave revolt in Charleston, South Carolina, but the conspiracy is not successful and he and 34 others are hanged.

1831

Nat Turner, who regarded himself as an agent of God to lead his people out of slavery, heads a slave rebellion in Southampton County, Virginia, in which 55 whites are killed; Turner is captured and executed. The revolt ended the false belief that slaves were either happy with their lives as they were or were too submissive to rebel. Abolitionist William Lloyd Garrison founds *The Liberator*.

1831-61

Around 75,000 slaves escape to freedom in the Northern states and

Canada using the Underground Railroad.

1838

Frederick Douglass escapes from slavery on September 3.

1839

The slaves aboard the *Amistad* mutiny, and reach Long Island; they are later defended by former president John Quincy Adams and win their freedom in a Supreme Court case, which freed them and returned them to Africa.

1845

Frederick Douglass publishes his autobiography *The Narrative of the Life of Frederick Douglass: An American Slave,* and it becomes a best seller.

1847

Douglass founds an antislavery newspaper, *The North Star*, which is later renamed *Frederick Douglass's Paper.*

1849

Escaped slave Harriet Tubman becomes a conductor on the Underground Railroad.

1850

Compromise of 1850, written by Henry Clay, diffuses tension between the free and slave states in the Union. Part of the compromise is the passage of another Fugitive Slave Act mandating that the federal government support the capture of escaped slaves and that fugitive slaves could not testify on their own behalf, nor were they permitted a trial by jury.

1852

Harriet Beecher Stowe publishes the antislavery novel *Uncle Tom's Cabin*; it becomes a best seller, and contributes to turning Northern states against slavery.

1854

The Missouri Compromise is repealed by Congress, and the Kansas-Nebraska Act creates Kansas and Nebraska as territories and allows the people of each territory to decide for themselves whether or not to allow slavery.

1857

The U.S. Supreme Court decides the Dred Scott case, ruling that Congress had no power to ban slavery in the territories, or areas that were not yet states, and that Scott had no right to file a lawsuit.

1859

Abolitionist John Brown and others take the law into their own hands and attack the federal arsenal at Harpers Ferry, Virginia (now West Virginia), on October 16, hoping that thousands of slaves would rise in rebellion; the raid failed and Brown was captured, tried, convicted, and hanged.

1860

Abraham Lincoln is elected president of the United States. On December 20, South Carolina secedes from the Union.

1861

The American Civil War begins.

1863

President Lincoln declares the Emancipation Proclamation, which freed all slaves in the Confederate states.

1864

Congress officially repeals both of the Fugitive Slave Acts on June 28.

1865

On April 9, Union general Ulysses S. Grant accepts Confederate general Robert E. Lee's surrender in Appomattox, Virginia, and the Civil War ends. Congress passes the Thirteenth Amendment to the Constitution and it is ratified on December 6, putting an end to slavery.

GLOSSARY

ABOLISH To do away with completely or put an end to something.

ABOLITIONIST A person who is in favor of putting an end to slavery.

ARDOR Great eagerness or zeal.

COMPROMISE A settlement of a dispute by each party giving up some demands.

DISENFRANCHISE To prevent a person or a group of people from having the right to vote.

EMANCIPATION The act of freeing someone from slavery.

ERADICATE To eliminate or destroy.

FANATICISM Excessive enthusiasm or intense devotion.

FREE STATE A state where slavery was prohibited before the Civil War.

INDENTURED SERVANT A person bound to an employer for a limited number of years.

INHERENT Belonging to or being a part of the nature of a person or thing.

MIDDLE PASSAGE The forced voyage of enslaved Africans across the Atlantic Ocean to the Americas.

MULATTO A person of mixed white and black descent.

MUTINY A situation in which a group of people refuse to obey orders and try to take control away from the person who commands them.

PARADOX A person or thing having qualities that seem to be opposites.

PROCLAMATION Something that is announced publicly or declared formally.

RATIFY To give legal or official approval to something.

REPRESS To subdue or put down by force.

RHETORIC Language that is not honest, sincere, or meaningful.

SLAVE NARRATIVE An account of the life, or major portion of the
    life, of a fugitive or former slave, either written or orally related
    by the slave personally.

STATUTE A law put into effect by the legislative branch of a gov-
    ernment.

STRIDENT Sounding harsh and unpleasant.

FOR MORE INFORMATION

Abraham Lincoln Presidential Library and Museum

212 North 6th Street

Springfield, IL 62701

(217) 558-8844

Website: http://www.illinois.gov/alplm

Lincoln's presidential library and museum holds extensive documents and records relating to Lincoln's personal life and presidency.

African American Civil War Memorial & Museum

1925 Vermont Avenue NW

Washington, DC 20011

(202) 667-2667

Website: http://www.afroamcivilwar.org

This memorial honors the service of more than 200,00 African American soldiers and sailors who fought for the Union. The museum relates the stories of the U.S. Colored Troops and African American involvement in the U.S. Civil War. The collection houses primary resources, and offers exhibitions and lectures on African Americans in the Civil War.

Buxton National Historic Site & Museum

21975 A. D. Shadd Road

North Buxton, ON N0P 1Y0

Canada

(519) 352-4799

Website: http://www.buxtonmuseum.com

The Buxton museum collects, preserves, and exhibits historical artifacts devoted to the Elgin (also known as Buxton) Settlement from its establishment in 1849 to the late 19th century, and celebrates the efforts of the Underground Railroad. It was one of four organized black settlements created in Canada.

Frederick Douglass National Historic Site

1411 W Street SE

Washington, DC 20020

(202) 426-5961

Website: http://www.nps.gov/frdo/index.htm

The National Park Service at Cedar Hill preserves the home and legacy of Frederick Douglass. It was built in the 1850s and restored beginning in 2004. It officially reopened for visitors in 2007.

Harriet Tubman Home

180 South Street

Auburn, NY 13021

(315) 252-2081

Website: http://harriethouse.org

Underground Railroad conductor Harriet Tubman's house in Auburn, which she established as a home for elderly blacks is open for public tours.

John Freeman Walls Underground Railroad Museum

932 Lakeshore Road 107, RR 3

Essex, ON N8M 2X7

Canada

(519) 727-6555

Website: http://www.undergroundrailroadmuseum.org

The historic site honors the workings of the Underground Railroad and includes educational tours conducted by many descendants of the original conductors of the Underground Railroad.

Museum of the African Diaspora

685 Mission Street

San Francisco, CA 94105

(415) 358-7200

Website: http://www.moadsf.org

This museum provides educational and public programs on the culture, history, and art of people of African descent within the United States.

National African American Archives and Museum

564 Dr. Martin Luther King Jr. Avenue

Mobile, AL 36603

(251) 433-8511

Website: http://www.naaamm.org

This history museum contains archival materials, artifacts (including shackles, leg irons, slave collars, and other artifacts used in slavery), and carvings involving the African American experience. It also holds a large oral history collection.

National Civil War Museum

One Lincoln Circle at Reservoir Park

Harrisburg, PA 17103

(717) 260-1861

Website: http://www.nationalcivilwarmuseum.org

Exhibits and displays that include artifacts, documents, and photographs concerning Civil War battles and events can be viewed in the museum.

Old Slave Mart Museum

6 Chalmers Street

Charleston, SC 29401

(843) 958-6467

Website: http://www.charleston-sc.gov

This site relates the story of Charleston's role in the slave trade by presenting tours of the building and site where slave sales occurred until 1863.

WEBSITES

Because of the changing nature of Internet links, Rosen Publishing has developed an online list of websites related to the subject of this book. This site is updated regularly. Please use this link to access the list:

http://www.rosenlinks.com/AAE/Slave

BIBLIOGRAPHY

Aronson, Marc, and Marina Budhos. *Sugar Changed the World: A Story of Magic, Spice, Slavery, Freedom, and Science.* New York, NY: Clarion Books, 2010.

Bailey, Diane. *The Emancipation Proclamation and the End of Slavery in America* (A Celebration of the Civil Rights Movement). New York, NY: Rosen Publishing Group, 2015.

Bradford, Sarah. *Harriet Tubman: The Moses of Her People.* Mineola, NY: Dover Publications, 2004.

Herda, D. J. *The Dred Scott Case: Slavery and Citizenship* (Landmark Supreme Court Cases). Rev. ed. Berkeley Heights, NJ: Enslow Publishers, 2010.

Johnson, Claudia Durst. *Slavery in Narrative of the Life of Frederick Douglass* (Social Issues in Literature). Farmington Hills, MI: Greenhaven Press, 2014.

McNeese, Tim. *The Abolitionist Movement: Ending Slavery* (Reform Movements in American History). New York, NY: Chelsea House Publishers, 2007.

Nardo, Don. *The Atlantic Slave Trade* (Lucent Library of Black History). Farmington Hills, MI: Lucent Books, 2007.

Nardo, Don. *Slavery through the Ages* (World History). Farmington Hills, NY: Lucent Books, 2014.

Schraff, Anne E. *The Life of Frederick Douglass: Speaking Out Against Slavery* (Legendary African Americans). Berkeley Heights, NJ: Enslow Publishers, 2014.

Schraff, Anne E. *The Life of Harriet Tubman: Moses of the Underground Railroad* (Legendary African Americans). Berkeley Heights, NJ: Enslow Publishers, 2014.

Steele, Philip. *Documenting Slavery and Civil Rights* (Documenting History). New York, NY: Rosen Publishing Group, 2010.

Sterngass, Jon. *Frederick Douglass* (Leaders of the Civil War). New York, NY: Chelsea House Publishers, 2009.

Taylor, Yuval, ed. *Growing Up in Slavery: Stories of Young Slaves Told by Themselves.* Chicago, IL: Chicago Review Press, 2007.

Woog, Adam. *The Emancipation Proclamation: Ending Slavery in America* (Milestones in American History). New York, NY: Chelsea House Publishers, 2009.

INDEX